Travellers Gather Dust and Lust

Poetry

Gabriel Awuah Mainoo

Edited by Macpherson Okpara

Cover art

Mwanaka Media and Publishing Pvt Ltd,
Chitungwiza Zimbabwe
*
Creativity, Wisdom and Beauty

i

Publisher: Mmap
Mwanaka Media and Publishing Pvt Ltd
24 Svosve Road, Zengeza 1
Chitungwiza Zimbabwe
mwanaka@yahoo.com
www.africanbookscollective.com/publishers/mwanaka-media-and-publishing
https://facebook.com/MwanakaMediaAndPublishing/

Distributed in and outside N. America by African Books Collective
orders@africanbookscollective.com
www.africanbookscollective.com

ISBN: 978-1-77906-501-8
EAN: 9781779065018

©Gabriel Awuah Mainoo 2019

DISCLAIMER
All views expressed in this publication are those of the author and do not necessarily reflect the views of *Mmap*.

iii

Dedication

Ω .... Ω

This book is dedicated to the God of art, people of love and London, especially Paul E Pinnock family and friends because they made it happen.

Acknowledgements

Glory to the God of wisdom, love and art. It's been a long walk from the struggles. I express sincere gratitude to everyone who made this collection a success: Paul E Pinnock, family and friends, Writers Space Africa, African literature, Gertrude Kasseneh, Eric Tetteh, Beatrix Yaa Mensah, Nyashadzashe Chikumbu, Adjei Ajei-Baah Martin Egblewogbe, Sandra O Etubiebi, Tendai Rinos Mwananka, Francisca Nyarko, Kofi Dzogbewu, Macpherson Okpara, and all members of my team. Thank you for being the power in my windmill.

Grateful acknowledgment is due the publishers of the respective journal, volume, magazine and exhibition in which four of the poems in this anthology foremost appeared: Writers space Africa, Ghana writes literary journal and Poetry leaves exhibition, Waterford in the township of Michigan U.S.A.

God bless.

Endorsements

"As I take a glance on the title and cover of this breathtaking collection, it makes me feel like I am going to travel, through the lives, times and places of others, and their escapades or adventures and experience the world through poetry. The picture itself tells you of adventure. In this book, you'll be wandering in the feelings, frustrations and happiness of the poet, his inhabitants and beyond. It has a good flair for poetry. The cover does invoke an air of poetry, such that with greater finesse, it should stir a hunger to dig in."

Sandra Oma Etubiebi (Writers Space Africa, Nigeria)

"'Travellers Gather Dust and Lust' is a modern concoction of poems that takes the reader on a journey to explore snow in Africa through a cascade of darkness at noon time. The collection tells you that when you see the African abroad, they may just be on a pilgrimage of love and lullabies. Indeed, Gabriel Awuah Mainoo offers this collection as a form of libation, to cleanse your feet of all the dust you have gathered on your travels."

Kofi Dzogbewu (Writers project of Ghana)

Table of Contents

Foreword

The first thing that strikes a reader of any piece of work is its title. The title of Gabriel Awuah Mainoo's 'Travellers Gather Dust and Lust' gives a glimpse of the state of mind of the creator as he wrote the poems, in which he strikingly shows a great sense of artistic rebelliousness through the form and style he uses to paint the images that dot their landscape . The poet's skill in raising his concerns marks him as a lyricist extraordinaire.

In this debut collection of his poems, A.M.Gabriel writes with gentle affection, rich humor and a deep understanding of the lyrical form and African problem. His tone is strikingly optimistic although ironically he addresses a deep, heavy and burdening subject matter of disintegration of the African plain and its individual. With the precision of a neurosurgeon, he makes use of humor to carefully satirize the blind incompetence of the African masses dying of thirst yet their feet are submerged in water. This being the case of looking to the west, yet Africa is blessed with an abundance of resources (both human and natural). In the opening poem, 'Africa and snow' the poet writes:

> "...*this is how we die— Africa,*
> *Suffocating*
> *Suffocating...*"

.

The writer does not only show aptitude in tackling the problems in his native Ghana, but through his universally appealing form, style and way of description, he also shows great mastery of detail. In

'High above Zimbabwe', he describes the scene of Zimbabwe's current struggle and their courage to counter such predicaments as one who has been there. Thus, putting himself in one shoe with the victims. He writes:

> *"Even as the gale that move rocks sneezed,*
> *That is when their spirits grew manfully*
> *These fearless boys—*
> *All—singing Marley's 'one love'*
> *And their joyful hearts*
> *Rising high like their undaunted kites*
> *Soaring high*
> *Soaring higher*
> *High above the head of heaven".*

The subject matter of A.M.Gabriel varies in scope, grappling with the world at hand. He acts as a shepherd not as a hunter coming down from the mountain descending to wrestle every lion that prey on his flock, and as a poet of the people fighting every challenge as it comes from all directions. The lyrical pessimism of his poetry does not only reduce the African problem to its darkest bits but also offers hope; the rising of a brighter sun. He writes, in his master piece 'Dreadlocks',

> *"You see these things on my head*
> *Hanging idly like rags?*
> *Each is a totem:*
> *Of despair, of laughter of music and liberation*
> *Of beauty, of harmony, of fidelity and love refined…"*

Astonishingly, in his piece, "red what green'," this poet of illimitable affection goes to the extent of sympathizing with the soulless traffic light;

"Yet, you shed some unseen tears at noon,
Well, Sorry for the threat that nature bring—
Because I am aware of your agony
I know of the stinging night,
The tormenting thunder and the stabbing rain…"

Because he believes everything that has importance must be treated well with utmost care. This collection shall not survive its purpose if I clear the cobwebs on the readers' mind. Hence, let us jump onto the wheel and travel through times, happiness, thoughts, struggles, culture and frustrations of the poet. "It is only the writer and reader who live twice and perhaps some more" A.M. Gabriel. Thus experiencing your actual life and going into adventure(s).

Nyashadzashe   Chikumbu,   Zimbabwe   (Mystery   Publishers

Africa and snow

Mother is a world over-filled with gold
But anytime we want to make her a beautiful ornament
We travel across for glittering snow
And when her beautiful artifact tends dying
It melts gently
Slowly—
Each mighty drop completing an ocean
Drowning the children
Diluting the oil fields
And the wrath of ocean gales— wiping ancestral scars
Falling off our mighty trees
From cocoa
And coffee
To the last root of the cotton tree
Leaving us a cold river for the frozen crops
This is how we die—Africa
Suffocating
Suffocating
Africa, this is how we die.

Sentimental Synonyms

Stars you're fire
Fire you're red
Red you're greed
Greed you're Africa
Africa you're black
Black you're death
Death you're victory
Victory you're white
White you're joy
Joy you're life
Life you're art
You're the end art/
You're the beginning
Art you're Life
Life you're joy
Joy you're white
White you're victory
Victory you're death
Death you're black
Black you're Africa
Africa you're greed
Greed you're red
Red you're fire
Fire you're stars.
    Stars you're a distant mirror beholding our destiny.

Afrikana

Oh, you've forgotten this familiar voice so soon?
I am the laborer you employed on your snow field
When your frozen farm could not stand
I was he, who brought you loam from my mother's graveyard
The lurking waves are near
I am come knocking the moonlight door
It is me, the Afrikana
Will you open Sir?
Or just look me at the window and chide me once more.

Oh, landlord, you've forgotten this dark child so soon?
I am the tenant you welcomed into your garage
As your kitten took my place in the guest room
I have come with a basket of thorns woven by my people
For a share of what solely belongs to my ancestors
I am come knocking the moonlight door
It is me, the Afrikana
Will you open Sir?
Or just look me at the window
And hide me in your balcony.

It is me, the Afrikana
I am come on mother's last errand
With a golden necklace handsomely beaten from her shackles
I am come with your cross Sir
Knocking, knocking
It is me, the Afrikana

Will you open the moonlight door?

The grim reaper

We come, with those old broken familiar placards
High on the b/rattling ground
With prayers scribbled in the redness of scabrous skins
The cameras, the parasites, the soldiers— all present
But we did not come to war
We came, long defeated by regrets and strangling decisions.

We plead to die—thus our victory be
Gentle death hurts
A vessel that drowns you each day
Madly roller-coasting your soul dreams and spirit.

Reaper, you have failed to be our G/god
Long before Israel leaped the red sea
In the newspapers yesterday
I learnt you're a street sweeper in Canaan
And a reaper in Africa and whatever dark corn you winnow
A pretty chaff runs astray from your doorstep
If you should have trotted
Under the sick bridges and streets long after elections
You'd have seen flying mist of chaff
Eclipsing the dreams of Ghanaian youths.

Fine, enough, excuse our nosiness

We also know you're a scrap dealer in Dubai
And a night engineer in Africa
In the dim mirrors of the day
You interlock the hose of your lawns
Into the pores of our withered skins
And every beauty you behold on adventure
Is only great for the one
Whom you reciprocate your nakedness with.

BI-BO Black inside black outside

I liked her/ because she was dark and dirty/ and I was black and dirtier/ whenever she wore white/ I hated it/ because she looked multicolored, scabrous, masked—like a trickster/ you wouldn't know her true beauty/ her origin/whether she belonged here or beyond/or found in some slave boat/ she was a photocopy/ a true thing behind an inferior background/ yet, I hated it whenever she wore black/ because men looked her through their hearts/ the blackness, her scars, her faith, her madness, her dirtiness, her flimsiness, her sexiness, her flaws/ they harmonized with her skin— and she became all dark and true.

Infant rain

Back in the flooding streets of Accra
We'd run in the rain
Far from the distance between
Our frustrations and hunger
We'd throw stones onto ceilings and trees
Which we never knew would fiercely come back at us one day.

Footless as we ran
Along those thorny paths
Our fears and feelings sank into oblivion
With eyes keenly on the game
Hunting the homeless crows for the meager meal
Hungry and light as we were
Like a wandering leaf
We'd go anywhere
Anywhere the rude wind carried us.

And then we'd go
Far beyond the misery a child could see
We'd hear 'kpooo'...
And we'd love to know more
O, it was some pregnant men on the cross

And then we'd be happy their very blood atoned the land
Not because we had dead heart as theirs.

Whatever killing must be killed
It was justice at the firing square

Killing those killing the country
Killing what the country did not like
Killing what was killing the country
And then we'd mount our shirts on sticks
Singing 'hosanna
Hosanna Rawlings...'
Ah! How I wish to be a child again
To be beaten by one infant rain.

Of love and covenant

I looked at you uncertain
In the blurriness of my tears
You soared into the circling blues upon a man-made bird
Locking your shadow beneath the yellowish shade of summer
You soared
In a far distant
Where these fingers can no more reach their old rooms
Leaving an angel of river die of thirst
One who beholds you as light amidst every dark bend of his world
He dies of lurve
Of dreadful dreams
And longing fever.

If tomorrow finds me despite the malady
I'll find that familiar path we used to walk yonder Winneba
And seek the flame of covenant from your kin's abode
At my exit
I shall gather a hand full of dust of your mother's last footprint
Plead with your father's tear and build a titanic wall
Shielding this covenant.

I know you love purple and roses
Rooted deep in the wearied dust of our feet
I shall plant you roses of purple
From the realm of an imaginary garden
A yard no man has made footprints upon
I will not forget where you fought your mighty wars
On this bloodless field of spins and aces.

I shall gather dust of your past
Unite droplets of my sweat and mould a relic of you
And then I'll find you, wherever you can be in Arkansas
Your sweet fragrance will lead me there
Yes, I'll know where to find you
Within the golden walls of Henderson
Where you concealed the lust of a Ghanaian boy
That is where I'll mould a relic of you
We will reignite the covenant
And beneath its rising embers
With the last beat of clay
I'll raise a relic of a living warrior
High upon the shoulders of Henderson.

Avarice

Cat and mouse
Mouse in power
Cat the opposition.

Both are the thirsty fishes
In sweet oceans
Reaching the pauper's
Last drop of filthy water.

Absurdity, Insanity.

Father speaks of Mother's beauty

Son, it was a year I cannot recall
A year somewhat withered from my tree of memory
Somewhere after autumn
When the tooth of winter had learnt to gnaw
And round the sweet flaming woods
We sat b'neath the sheening eye of heaven.
Son! I could only recall
Something pretty and oval man calls moon
And the moment
Your mother's pride called to a heavenly duty
To swap the darling stars of heaven
Son, I could only recall your mother's beauty
At a glimpse of a lively throng of bouquet
As your mother stood as lily
Bopping amidst winter's tooth.

A night before

You should have told me of your vain voyage
I only had a clue you'd go in the dark
I took the dawn as night
And the night as dawn
Yet I would have eclipsed the sun
For you to walk through
But you decided to walk your way
Not even with a kiss
A kiss of betrayal
You went that way
This way over the crossbar.

This lane you have taken
Until I rehearse your footprints
I'm afraid we'll never share corns again
Because this path you've chosen
Only a one-way road—
Even if time and tides weren't on your side
This is not how swift you should cleave
Not this way, hurriedly over the crossbar.

If you should meet what your might cannot stand
I know there'll be no victory
Even so I am your acolyte
The coward to wear the cannon

This is not how you should cleave
When we have not reaped what we watered with our tears
This is not how you should cleave

When we have not shared what we'll winnow with our breath.
This is not how you should have cleaved
Not this way—hurriedly over the cross bar.

Just the dream

Yonder these Ashaiman streets
Sometimes a sudden grief would come to me
It might be anger
A jealous feeling within
Anytime I recall the success of a renowned bastard friend
It seems to me that the world will come to darkness tomorrow
But yonder these familiar streets
When I see some hopeless men
Still hopeful
Some crippled friends outpacing wheels
Those who cannot see, running towards the trophy
An instant bliss entangles my heart
Then I'd laugh to myself and bless my good name.
"The dream,
Boy— just the dream"

Yonder these Ashaiman streets
Sometimes a sudden grief would come to me
It might be hunger
A yearning feeling towards the goal
Anytime I recall the success of a renowned bastard friend
It seems to me that my dreams have had a premature bond with dust
But yonder these familiar streets
Whenever I recall the utterings of one preacher man
Who talked of ancient instances
Of Sarah, of Abraham, of prayers, of fortitude
Of Joseph, of colossal wars and heroes and undaunted men
An instant wing of zeal entangles my limbs
Just like the fearless eagle

I'd light up with courage and eagerly fly to the dream
"The dream,
Boy— just the dream"

Taunt

Here I scribble again not to tease.
The wounded hearts I scribble to ease
Their apparent struggles and the undisclosed
And scars which cannot be dabbed off after their wails
With my harmless spear I cause these scars to die.

To those tricksters
Who in Yahweh's name fake holiness and genuineness
And from their kitchenette use cooking oil to bless
Blind ye all!
Who are unable to discern darkness from light of heaven
Deaf dogs, with tortured tongue, unable to bark at the worst
May the wrath of the maker mar your peace!

Now to those country shepherds; the gentle thieves
Who deliberately mistake fidelity for incompetence
And behind the equal sign
Their outcome, disgusting as never
And when aggrieved tongues turn a desert
Into our mouths
They make their pregnant wives spittoon leak.

To those country servants
Who are weak, not strong and able
Yet unwilling to give way to younger strengths
May I ask, "If greed will forever be your creed?"
Retire, go, and console your toothless wife!
Your dancing bones deserve rest
In a hurry to be fed by a hungry pest

Go! Since you've given your worst;
Leave the affairs to younger strengths.

And to the worst
Those traitors, who photocopy justice to seem original
Their sickness isn't hunger, but what makes them abuse hunger
Will the poor man's sick fowl you took as bribe
Quench the lantern that upholds justice?
Or should a tin of milo make you betray the truth?
Look into your senses and find out if you are well.
Your deeds don't deserve heaven
Tonight I throw my spear not to stab but to taunt
And if by day you miss the outdooring of the sun
At your arrival in hell
Tell death I need employment
Not to be a murderer but a harmless spear
Piercing smiling evils.

ZERO FIVE
LOVE FORTY

0,5/ 0,40
In and out of these cones
I tirelessly sprint and spin on this base
I wonder not
The service court repels my aces
Rivers reject me when I abuse their path
The flame is begging to die in my eyes
I refuse to toast my flaccid manhood
I have died more times than I've lived.

While a little boy I asked my father in manful tears
If I could be a soldier…

"Son, ask a thousand times
And the answers drowns you
Encrypt every score, every error and pain into the recycle bin
We know it's a clean trash…
Eat it, drink it, smear it, sex it your way— it is called ART
Learn to withstand sorrows young
Then rehearse the way to cry in your head
Drum it, dance it, shout it your way—it is called MUSIC
Live each day painfully for tomorrow
Because losing a family or a family losing you
Is an illusory comedy of real characters
Learn to live the madness—it is called LIFE".

When Christmas Falls

When Christmas fall by your balcony
Up, up to your neighbors
'Haps to Abe, and bid him
"A merry Christmas and a happy chicken"
And when Abe, had had a sweet night
And dreamt of Santa Claus, of red, of white
Of glamorous furnishings, of pretty fireworks
And the grace Christmas brings
Of church, of jingling bells, of hymns, of carols
Of praises, of melodies and the gratification music gives
Of chicken wings, of bottles, of wine, of aromas
Of candies, of pavlova, of diabetes
And cavity after New Year
Of gold, of myrrh, and of frankincense
Of thankfulness and reconciliation
Of stars, of mangers and the success of the three sages
Of an infant emperor, long birthed in Bethlehem
And the merry of a new year's eve
And of how he, Abe rendered to the poor
Like him, Abe, go dream, love, learn to give
Find cheer, but friend, you better be wary.

O Come you little Bird

Bleaker nights gently fade away
Upon the mountain chest
And the beautiful days gladly vacate
O'er the soundless clapping waters
A sweet hymn dies right at the window side
Amid a greener landscape
Down an ageless colorful foliage
As a grey folk wakes to solitude.
Ah! Where hath mi wondrous singer wander?
O, mi little humming bird
Why hath thee ditched mi spirit
Upon the blankness of the lonely night?
Come you, such wondrous creature
For mi spirit yearns for thine nocturnal rhymes.

High above Zimbabwe

And sweetly freedom came—
And some boys down Greendale
Soaring kites high above the chest of Zimbabwe
And each bird that flew beneath the stiff rivers above
And below the happiness of the boys
Wondered—
How Zimbabwe has reached this acme
And as the rage of heaven grew dim
The cloud greatly wept
Then these boys
Recalling the blessing that rain brings
Still playing—
Swimming cheerfully in the deadly deluge
Even as the gale that move rocks sneezed
That is when their spirits grew manfully
These fearless boys—
All—singing Marley's 'one love'
And their joyful hearts
Rising high like their undaunted kites
Soaring high
Soaring higher
High above the head of heaven.

The world's a Tennis Court

The world is a parted rectangular lawn,
With two gentlemen apart,
One at a side
And the other at another aside
Each man born a conqueror
Has his ways bounded by oppositions
The prime enemy, the net, being a perilous barrier
At the wars, every incoming ball is a challenging instance
But whosoever learns to win before the war
Counters defeat —holds a greater fraction to his destiny.

There may be traitors —a racket broken to the enemy's advantage
And the inner man —the confidence within
Whose zeal in any day could die like a melting butter
When rallies come long
These feet may tremble
With the arm hardened like wax
But do not give up so soon
Should you seek a favorable wall to lean upon
Not the lines men or the fallible umpire —our greatest betrayal

Who by external influence may foul the virtue of fidelity.
No matter how beautiful the swings seem
In no case will all commendations be handsome and pleasing.
There's always one man with a scornful applause in the stands.

Is the arm broken?

Stiff and hardened like wax?
Unable to make the ace?
Like death, this is how injury strangles
Exiting us from this rectangular field
Of spins
Of volleys
Of slices
Of adversaries
Of beautiful swings and aces.
This is how death comes
Vainly plucking our unripe dreams.
This is how death comes
Game—
Set—
And a sorrowful match.

Afri-lad

Africa's tissue is clasped intimately to your soul
Do not wander afar
Else Africa will fall amiss.
Do not look beyond rivers
Honor is here.
Or is it fame?
Luxury or pleasure?
All lies abyss the sanctuary of our struggles
Solely bestowed to the youth
Who endures the plight
To foresee Africa's glory.
Who'll harvest the sweet crops
 When our folks smear wrinkles?
Who'll clack the cannon
When foes invade?
Who'll discover the treasure beneath
The bluntness of our cutlasses
When you're away?
Soul brother,
Do not go far from home,
You may look different abroad.
Carve the land that gave you identity.
Do not leave Africa in the malady of grief,
Do not! —Our bond is deep!

Better to bitter

Potentates—

We told you we were hungry

You gave us lime

Yet we assumed satisfaction.

We requested fidelity

Then you added water to the lime

Did you ever know the war you brought into mouths?

Cascade

Sprinkle over my soul
When my heart is pale,
Flood the strife,
Enliven the life,
And if a mocking madness rages the mind
Gush fiercely abyss
And unshackle the spirit
Cascade!

Cascade!
You gentle flowing light,
Show me the way
When dark shadows of the greyed years
Reap thorns upon my age.
My days were darker nights
When my life was full of leprosy.

Cascade!
Engulf the awfulness of yore,
You faithful tabernacle!
Cascade!

Cascade!
When the hills go silent
And the night cast shadows aloft
I'll lay the heaviest wool to snore beside
The sacred waters
Perhaps when misfortune raids my home
This heart shall briskly serve the sting
And its scars

Be swamped beneath rocks.
Cascade.

When you see the African abroad

When you see the collier's son abroad
With his pigment like your heart
Pardon, pardon, sir!
Do not show him the gun.
Do not let him know
That both skins are different potteries of one God,
Just tell him:
Both are also the fetuses of mid winter's joy
Else he may abhor his pride.
When you see the collier's son abroad
Do not be too witty on him
Else you'll become a fool.
You may give him the shovel for vain labor
Aftermath if he's still stronger than you,
Do not keep him as gold
Neither should you tell him to come home
Just say to him:
Afro boy —your footprints have gathered flames.

A moment with Franca

Ah, what is that thing
Knocking on the head of the ceiling?
"Oh, it might be the bad children throwing stones".
Franca, listen with a generous ear
Perhaps it is the heavens urinating
"Oh heavens, you so nasty".

It wasn't long after the rain came
We had had a lovely chat
About books and headaches
And a black life abroad
And how sweet and kind Americans are
We discussed rackets and balls
Her favorite was babolat and I too
We talked about tears and laughter
Autumn and pretty flowers
Roses were her choice and daffodil was mine.

As she recalled a sweet moment
I realized how beautiful spring was
She promised to bring spring to Accra
I pinched myself so hard
And laughed out that illusory wish through my arse
We scheduled to talk about love another day
Because it is a handsome creeping flame
That rises from the base.
I asked about Marcel and Gabriel
And how smooth they are making for the acme

Neither did I forget Darko, Kpodo nor Ofoe
She said:
"Dear, they are alive and well.
Just a distance wide like the ocean separates their shadows".

She showed gratitude to NMMI
And how glad she was
Making it to Henderson
Silence came—
Then she wept a while
Because her memories with Mikyla and Becsy
Were fading soon.

So quickly after rain
The rainbow had gracefully curled across the blues
We stood at the balcony
Talked about chameleons and rainbows
And where the homeless birds will perch tonight.

Ashes of my race

There is this ancestral tree
Standing amid our home
Whenever morning comes
With the sun creeping above our brows
We march piously with sanctified soles
From the first to the last head of our race
From the last to the departed child to be born
Filing past this mighty tree, once, twice and once more
Chorusing, "Odomankoma—we thank you
"Asase Yaa—Adehyiema are grateful".

This mighty tree, our sanctuary
This tree— shielding our sickly huts
With its eagle-like wings sprout out
Like a silvery cloud upon our roofless home
This very tree too, our contentment
If awful harvest comes
We gladly eat from its rotten bough
Yet, find a handsome heart to say
"Odomankoma—we thank you
Asase Yaa—Adehyiema are grateful".

This tree couldn't deny us joy
Whenever Opanyin Mainoo
Carved the drum and flute out of it
Music became a moment god
Our wonderful women—
Winding

Dancing
Gesturing the weave of a golden kente in the air—
Flaunting their curves to the sonorous clinks of diamond beads
Bending
And—
Rising magnificently
Like a sweet smoke crinkling out of a royal horn
Then our gentlemen too
Gracefully—flapping carefully their arms
Like they've got golden eggs in their armpits.

Until one night when the moonlight tales
Had died in the smoldering fire
This tree—standing alone
Shedding a dark tear of tomorrow's sorrow
And its root leading to the gullet of our route
Strangled!
This tree, withering—weeping more.
I, seeing strangers over the coast
Recalled how these fallible gods came
Discovered what Odomankoma might have forgotten
Fell this mighty tree
Carved it into taverns and gambling tables
Brought us tales of their own
Of how winter came, and summer, and spring, and autumn
And our Anansesɛm, preserved
In the museum of their everyday dreams.

Calendars

Age is a dying flame
Rising solemnly yonder the blues like frankincense
And no smoke rises astray
Nor descend to soar again.

Tick —
The sun smiles here
Good morn angelic coals
How now Africa?
When will bountiful harvest come?

Tack—
The sun piddles there
Good eve Eurasia
How good was summer?
Let me know how sweet the chamomile did grow.
Tick tack—tick tack

Life is also a dying candlelight
And sometimes to the affluence a melting rock
And when soon every man's flare brings
Him a perpetual eve
His miserable end— be gathered as wax
Left to darkness and to worms.

IN AN AFRICAN'S DREAM
UNKNOWN VOICES IN VOICES

There is a wall parting us   color?
You are made of stars and fire   let's call the difference beauty
and repulsion
In Africa riches are better than a good name   only those who
know the irony survive
Often the problem knows us better   on this land,
you kill a problem, you kill a man
So we finish the business in the rising incense   it doesn't end there,
the blood revives
D o g (s); dependent on G/god (s)   this is how we live in
this cathedral
Tell me more   the story is with you,
my scars; your guilt
Who are you?   I'm a growing
mustard seed in Nile's slivery face
The memories are broken in your gullet   we know, we pass the spoon
through our anus
Look into the mirror and help me laugh   stranger, the stigma laughs
back at us
           I abhor the fun
Rising into leading rays of hope, I seal the deadly crevices with my
father's face.

I'll sing, I'll dance

Halt de Jazz—Mr. Armstrong
And tell me where I come from
I find history in ya rhythm.

Halt de bla-bo dance—lady Blackamoor
And tell me how we got here dancing
I find mystery in ya steps.

Now rest de fingers— Mr. Duke
And tell me why you casting out de strife
I find a teasing misery in ya chords too.

Today I'll sing—I'll dance
Whatever this dance be
I shall dance to shake off the fetters
Today I'll sing—I'll dance
However this song be
I shall sing for new dawn bliss.
I'll dance— I'll sing
I'll sing—I'll dance
To bring to cinders the pain of the past.

Mi lady's infiniteness

Sorry Africa
You cannot part my woman's breast with me
Because she is an immortal—an angelic being
She is plump black
She is plump dark
She is an elegant black dark coal.

Forgive me Europe
Only four legs on the cold linen at a time sire
You cannot feel my woman with me
Because her heat, her vibes
Repels the combustible wrath of summer
She is a warm fire—
A gentle glinting flame.

A boundless treasure has eluded you, Asia
Mi lady's worth, not the gambling tables
Now go bid the gambling heads they've lost the gambit
And submit them the truth that she's mine alone
She's not your meager bullions—she's a world of mines
Your sweetest cologne—not even half her whiff—
She's all graceful things the Highest Man has given—
She's a soothing rising tang of ylang-ylang
Incomparable!

Until wealth will know it is riding on season's wheel
By man's final exit
Death shall know his unfavorable worth
By then beauty's glory will long be gone

But as my upper lines still live to bear
That you—
You—
You mi lady
You're the soul of an undying star.

The day after freedom

It wasn't about how long we've been in shackles
It wasn't about how many times we've said
"Yes sah, yes sah masa"
"awil" while unwilling
It wasn't about how long
We've being starved from drums and harmonies
And the longing hurtful songs
Decayed beneath our woeful tongues.

It was about this beautiful morning after rain
When mother returned from the dreamland
Looked up the heavens and smiled like the sunshine
And said "Kwame negro, the rainbow has come
We do not have to beg to die again"
Until the sea becomes cheerful

They might have not gone far
Let's punctuate our joyful laughter
They might be lurking behind the victory walls
For a moment let us go back
Put on the shackles, and learn to laugh in them.

For a moment let us go back, learn to say
"Yes sir, no master
How about that?
What's your say?"
Then when we've learn to laugh bravely
We shall call them freedom songs
Sir, don't you want to leave our victory walls?

Perhaps our screams of joy might gnaw your lungs
You may leave sir, well, you may stay too
Our mother taught us to laugh— even on the war field.

A moment by the river side

When mi life hath seen enough of tormenting betrayals
I'll prefer to sit on the foamy rocks
B'neath the nature paradise
There, where the clement rivers doth cure
And watch the healing crystal waters delightfully bend
And sometimes, I'd love the rivers to solemnly curve along
With my pallid soul
Moping each scar of love denied.

Halt you sweet waters—thou may hear mi tragic tale
"I've loved with such an infinite heart like you waters
Friend's counsels were— but a sweet bane
Father's warmness was—but a titanic storm
Folks, thy promises were—but a never-born sun
Dim, dead and rotten in thy "D" figured paunch vault.

Mainoo, an endowed star like me;
When denials hath become a shadow b'neath my good name
Should the fine light
B'neath my glistening boon soon be vainly gone?
Hold me Ghana, Africa— I am the light in thy gloom

So you see, mi fine flowing friend
Every man's life is his own war
The kin is—but a liability
Our loved ones are—but our greatest weaknesses"
Nature may I be thy eternal companion?
In you I confidently confide in
As I steal a silent ear

I find life's music in thy miming
See, the airy flight there's pleasure in their gliding
The unflagging hangers, life is beautiful b'neath those trees.
Thy boundlessness hath taught me of man's eternal war
And in thy music I find my triumphant song
Somewhere the estuary where the ocean and tide gladly merge
Such gesture hath eagerly taught me to reconcile.
And at thy tributary, If you were a small stream
You'd reluctantly flow into a Lethe so grand
Such gesture too hath taught me of man's final exile
Teacher!
Until a long eve comes twice to me this day;
I shall be strong
I shall be strong!

By the road

 I lay my head on jagged stones
By the road I wake without folding my mat
Because roads can't be rolled.
By the road I wave the moon to death
On a desert belly
As hunger rant mournful poems
From the pulpit of my human intestines.

By the road I recline in a peaceful hell at night
With complaints of sleepless toads
Alongside thunderous hymns of four-wheel rides.

By the road
I've known gentle death
By the road
I've lived the life of a tortured lioness.
My life is of struggles
And struggles have walked near this road
Unless you do not chastise endurance
You can refuse to see
Beyond the land of the strangers.
Yet I have slept where the stars slept
As you did
And woke to the song of a morning thrush
As you did
And will lend my breath to the night
As you will do.

Yet I have lived to the opposite sweetness
Of your heavenly world
By the road; my dream is to be you
Swimming through the mud to safe curves
I hope for the blessings that fate dispenses.

Red what green

Hey you!
How long has your god
Forsaken you amid this cluttered road?
You were so fortunate
That Obronyi molded you without
Sunsum, honam and mogya.

I am aware there's bliss
In the smile of the morning sun
Yet, you shed some unseen tears at noon,
Well, sorry for the threat that nature bring—
Because I am aware of your agony
I know of the stinging night
The tormenting thunder and the stabbing rain.

I heard on the news that a man's shadow
Had rehearsed suicide after being dismissed by his superior
For being late to work— young man I know you're the reason.
On that same day
I learnt in the *Daily Graphic*
That a child went laughing all day
After being beaten
For being the first to report to school last
This very one too, young man— I know you're the reason.

Do your commanding eyes only trap wheels and obstruct?

Not sickness?
Death?
Could you not halt the deviant wind?
Or some moment or season that was too swift?
These all— my God can, He's able!

Poor boy
How long has your god
Forsaken you amid this cluttered road?
You were fortunate
That Obronyi molded you without
Sunsum, honam and mogya
Yet, I am aware of your anguish
Now go tell court how well
Government abuses you
Because you too—
You make an orderly nation.

Fall O child

Now fall
Fall unto the pillow o little child
Ev'n the homeless sun has found a lengthy wad;
A perching space b'hind the nocturnal shade
Tighter and tighter lock thy brow
A beautiful day in Accra swiftly dies away
So, hurry, hurry O dearest child
Else the soulless souls will come for you
From the ceiling they'll descend like spiders
And chastise the children that do not sleep.

Peace, O peace little child
Hush and fall unto the pillow
Ev'n the homeless sun has found a lengthy wad;
A perching space b'hind the nocturnal shade
Tighter and tighter lock thy brow
A beautiful day in Accra swiftly dies away
So hush, hush O dearest child
The Boogey man is fast at snore
Amid ev'ry child's dream he'll fiercely come
And hunt the children that often cry.

Fall to rest O darling child
Darkness has fallen o'er the parks and swings
Ev'n the homeless sun has found a lengthy wad;
A perching space b'hind the nocturnal shade
Tighter and tighter lock thy brow
A blissful day in Accra swiftly dies away

This world is a mean and tormenting field
Sometimes thy father's warmth is but a cub's abode
Here, to mama o lovely child
B'neath a mother's blanket is a fountain of solace.

The boy and his kite

If you take the fish out of the sea, there's still the sea
I for sure know you cannot take the sea out of the fish.
This reminds me of a growing boy
Along the boulevards of Streatham
At every birth of sunshine he'd fly a kite
Beyond where his cheerfulness should reach.

Each day he flew a different lovely flag
On the first day
He flew his white vest beyond boundaries of home
It returned, clean, just like it went—obedient.

On the second day
After the anthem from the morning birds
He flew the flag of his homeland
And his linen returned in blotches through the dying sunlight.

He flew a renowned flag on the third day
And it returned, fresher than before
Then he learnt
Wherever there's love, there is preference and disparity.

There were days he flew some twice
Yet, none returned
That was when this growing boy learnt to play in a bottle
And has known his sea has a barrier.

Along the boulevards of Streatham
Now unlike each day

He'd fly his grandpa's ageless blue and white polo stripes
And skillfully play in hissing circles of the wind
Right within the heart of Streatham.

Okada blues

It is famine in the homeland
My dying mother tells me to plough and plant
In a concrete yard of her womb
At sundown I leave for our master's dung
Our soil is dead b'neath skeletons of sheer incompetence
I do not want to return as a zero
For trophies made from native skulls
You know Nigeria and traffic
It is only green for the politician.

At sunset, descending our fallen sanctuary
We will ride to Amelicar
And fetch home whatever manure lying abyss their eminence
On arrival
I'll offer you Trump's testicles for Caesar's head.

Now, we will sneak through the pores of Mexico
And conspire with the guards
I know, wherever there's democracy
There's little stink
But if they seem too clean some gods,
We will steal into our skins
And zombie them with our juju
Alagbaraniwa
Alagbaraniwa
How much na, okada?
Our back is falling apart into deep crimson embers.

When You Refrain a Child from Growing

You met mother at ten/ and slashed her front at sixteen
Seventeen/ we couldn't conjure how fast you run onto the track of
capriciousness
Eighteen/ You baked her back
Nineteen/ society stripped off your towel in the market square
Twenty/ weeds came you weeded and yielded your third harvest
Each time it seemed there was a year you feared to be a man.

I'm seventeen/ you wrap me in diapers and clad me in fetters
Eighteen/ when everyone knew I was capable
You still carried me over those staircases
Nineteen/ you call me to the bedroom and ask me to come with my
back
Twenty/ you put three things on a red veil
Bible, condom and destiny
A woman asks me to undress and I quote her exodus chapter twenty
verse something...
Knowing very well time has a dying contract with lust.

At twenty six
If it should have been about manfulness and arms
I'd always prefer mother's sleekened skinny sleeve
And then flaunt my sexy bones in them.

Show me your heaven and fold that balloon into your skirt
I am ready to be a man
Get me an axe beside the bed and if father happens to sneak in
I'll show him I've been in the boyhood movies for too long.

The Visitation

A BROKENHEARTED WOMAN INVADES HOMES WITH
LEMON UNDER HER TONGUE
  PREACHING SELF-DISCIPLINE TO MEN

I asked if I could offer water
She swallowed her regrets and spat on God's face three times
Then I realized her war with men/

But how glad I was when you brought God to my doorstep
In your gleaming postiche
Suffocating the FATHER
The SON
And the HOLY GHOST in your shredded veil
I offered you a chair but you preferred my lap
That way you could preach with your body
Turning round around my pivot/
The moment, the rosary gazed—I
I lingered
My head
My mind
Gyrating like busy fan blades
I hold my soft stick so hard
That I wouldn't lash your holy ass to flames
I curse you for making me think like a sinner/
You asked my sins
I confessed you're my temptation
And I regretted making you leave this way

With your back facing desires /
Saintly sinister
Wonderfully winding in whorls
Hoh! It was a pretty eyesore
I should have just welcomed the way you came
Desperately meeting your madness/

Spins and death

You came
In circles
Winding
Twisting
Dangerously
Like a woman
Anytime I looked you with lust, you fled astray.

Again you came
Slowly
In turns
And turns
Innocent
Smiling like a playful boy with iron canines
This time you feigned a child and squeezed my testicles.

Often you arrive higher this way
At a completion of a parabola
Right at the base
Hurling us in-between coffins and graves
With a sicken essence
That we may die through struggles and still die again.

Akɛtesia

1990: the beautiful ones are not yet born.

 I arrived at your mother's doorstep
On the lead of a shooting star
With a thousand cowries
And a singing cockerel
A dear hunt of seven deer
And a golden handmade of maame Akua Akuaba's akuaba
If your mother's dark world was huge enough
To contain what I couldn't carry
I would have offered many things of land of beauty and love
Akɛtesia
Akɛtesia
I will be waiting you for a wife.

1991: The beautiful ones are born.

I arrived at your mother's doorstep
In laughter
On the lead of descending infant rays
Golden rains have fallen upon my seeds
Attaa maame
I learnt my harvest has yielded in manifolds
Whatever belongs to me must go with me
I will light my flame the way I want it glow
Not with fire, not with stones, not with coal,
Not in woods, not in strife

And you say she's too fresh for a toast?

2020: The beautiful ones are dying.

Akɛtesia
The last time I saw you was in the dreamland
You sent me to fetch fire in the rain
That was when I knew something was waning
Yet you should have professed how well you loved me that way
 And your mother hated me this way
And how well your mother loved me this way and you hated me
that way.

1970: the beautiful ones are dead and gone.

You've sent me to my birth again
Weeping
Weeping like a child yearning for alewa
I look like something grey you might not like
My harvest has been flooded by my very sweat
O, Akɛtesia
Akɛtesia
Akɛtesia.

2000 and...

The shooting star has fallen into the sea
I come to your house and see strange things
Whatever mellifluous I used to hear I hear no more
Decrescendo
Decrescendo
My singing cockerel slaughtered for the visitors

And the deer for the mourners
Akɛtesia you should have confessed you'll betray me this way
And how well your mother will betray me that way
The problem is...
You've always been too young for everything
To love
To be a wife
Even to die
Akɛtesia
Akɛtesia
You've been too young for everything.

The Pilgrimage

When I am hop
A step beyond your sight
Do not feign sweet tears upon my name
Oh Awuah awake
Mainoo awake
Your prickly dirges shall kill me more.

Until the sun blushes
On my path again
Do not convolute the prettiest
Wreath upon my grave—
These unworthy blossoms
They may mock me more.

Onua
When on the road to our wooden enclave
You find my leady cross
Greatly heavy upon my guilt
Do not be too swift to succor —
You too shall have a conference
With the pest tomorrow.

Onua
When you find me wobbling
On the other lane
Do not wail too sweetly
Just lay an honest hand
And spit the ancestral credo upon my grave.

Dreadlocks

You see these things on my head
Hanging idly like rags?
Each is a totem
Of despair, of laughter of music and liberation
Of beauty, of harmony, of fidelity and love refined
As these ropes gladly swing
To the incessant rhythm of the gale
There's this sudden putrid wind that comes
 Rushing violently into my nose
This reminds of decaying hands in government offices.

You see these things on my head
Hanging idly like rags?
My joy and all
If reggae sneaks through my chamber
With a new morn blushing upon my dreads
A petty madness comes
Then I do the jump
One leg high, one leg low
One hand high, one hand low
Shake off the dirt in my dreads
 And sing
"Jah, I am grateful for the abundant breath,
I thank you for my mother and Africa".

Glossary

Honam— the skin or the flesh.

Mogya— blood.

Obronyi— white man.

Sunsum— the spirit.

Asase Yaa— in appellation; goddess of land.

Adehyiema— native(s) of a town or clan.

Odomankoma— in appellation; the greatest (reference to God in the poem).

Kente— a brightly colored cloth consisting of separate strips sewn together.

Anansesɛm— Ghanaian folktales which is centered round the foolish-wise spider, Ananse.

Opanyin— an elder from a clan.

Onua— brother (son of the same parents as another person)

Akɛtesia— a young girl who has not yet reached marriage age.

Alagbaraniwa— "we are men of powers" (Yoruba).

Juju—a charm with supernatural powers.

Attaa maame/ntaa maame— mother of a twin or triplets.

Alewa— a round headed sweet with a stick which can be likened to lollipop.

Akuaba— a female playing doll normally carved from wood. (Akan traditional art).

Okada— a one passenger motto cycle.

Akua— a soul name given to a lady born on Wednesday.

Daily Graphic—the name of a Ghanaian-based newspaper.

Publisher's list

If you have enjoyed *Travellers Gather Dust and Lust* **consider these other fine books from Mwanaka Media and Publishing:**

Cultural Hybridity and Fixity by Andrew Nyongesa
The Water Cycle by Andrew Nyongesa
Tintinnabulation of Literary Theory by Andrew Nyongesa
I Threw a Star in a Wine Glass by Fethi Sassi
South Africa and United Nations Peacekeeping Offensive Operations by Antonio Garcia
Africanization and Americanization Anthology Volume 1, Searching for Interracial, Interstitial, Intersectional and Interstates Meeting Spaces, Africa Vs North America by Tendai R Mwanaka
A Conversation..., A Contact by Tendai Rinos Mwanaka
A Dark Energy by Tendai Rinos Mwanaka
Africa, UK and Ireland: Writing Politics and Knowledge Production Vol 1 by Tendai R Mwanaka
Best New African Poets 2017 Anthology by Tendai R Mwanaka and Daniel Da Purificacao
Keys in the River: New and Collected Stories by Tendai Rinos Mwanaka
Logbook Written by a Drifter by Tendai Rinos Mwanaka
Mad Bob Republic: Bloodlines, Bile and a Crying Child by Tendai Rinos Mwanaka
How The Twins Grew Up/Makurire Akaita Mapatya by Milutin Djurickovic and Tendai Rinos Mwanaka
Writing Language, Culture and Development, Africa Vs Asia Vol 1 by Tendai R Mwanaka, Wanjohi wa Makokha and Upal Deb

Ouafa and Thawra: About a Lover From Tunisia by Arturo Desimone

Thoughts Hunt The Loves/Pfungwa Dzinovhima Vadiwa by Jeton Kelmendi and Tendai Rinos Mwanaka

وَالغَمَام...ويَسهَرُ اللَّيْلُعَلَشَفَتي by Fethi Sassi

A Letter to the President by Mbizo Chirasha

Righteous Indignation by Jabulani Mzinyathi:

This is Not a Poem by Richard Inya

Blooming Cactus by Mikateko Mbambo

Soon to be released

Notes From a Modern Chimurenga: Collected Stories by Tendai Rinos Mwanaka

Tom Boy by Megan Landman

My Spiritual Journey: A Study of the Emerald Tablets by Jonathan Thompson

Rhythm of Life by Olivia Ngozi Osouha

School of Love and Other Stories by Ricardo Felix Rodriguez

Cycle of Life by Ikegwu Michael Chukwudi

Denga reshiri yokunze kwenyika by Fethi Sassi

Because Sadness is Beautiful by Tanaka Chidora

PHENOMENOLOGY OF DECOLONIZING THE UNIVERSITY: Essays in the Contemporary Thoughts of Afrikology by Zvikomborero Kapuya

INFLUENCE OF CLIMATE VARIABILITY ON THE PREVALENCE OF DENGUE FEVER IN MANDERA COUNTY, KENYA by NDIWA JOSEPH KIMTAI

https://facebook.com/MwanakaMediaAndPublishing/

Printed in the United States
By Bookmasters